D1143110

Is it about a Bicycle?

Thoughts for the day

OLIVER CRILLY

VERITAS

Published 2003 by
Veritas Publications
7/8 Lower Abbey Street
Dublin 1
Email publications@veritas.ie
Website www.veritas.ie

ISBN 1 85390 736 7

10 9 8 7 6 5 4 3 2 1

A catalogue record for this book is available from the British Library.

Designed by Bill Bolger
Printed in the Republic of Ireland by Betaprint Ltd, Dublin

*Veritas books are printed on paper made from the wood pulp of
managed forests. For every tree felled, at least one tree is planted,
thereby renewing natural resources.*

Contents

Introduction

I spent thirteen years of my life 'in the media' in Dublin, as an editor and publisher, and then as director of the Catholic Communications Institute, but it was only after I returned to Northern Ireland that I became involved in a personal way with radio and television. I remember the total stage-fright that I experienced when Fr Jim Skelly of the BBC involved me in a half-hour television interview as part of an inter-church series called *Perspectives*. During the interview I wanted a drink of water, but I couldn't reach out to lift the glass, because I knew my hand would shake uncontrollably. After that baptism of fire, cameras and microphones were never quite so intimidating. Although I worked on various programmes – Sunday morning studio services on radio, broadcast Masses, interviews, a

TV documentary in Irish on the Donegal writer Seosamh Mac Grianna, and press conferences on occasions like the 1981 hunger strikes and the 1997 Independent Review of Parades and Marches – I found that *Thought for the Day* became my favourite broadcasting experience.

Writing a piece for *Thought for the Day* is probably more like writing poetry than writing prose. In the first place, it is strictly limited in length, though by minutes and seconds rather than by number of lines. The length imposes a discipline which creates an economy of words. If the text has to be trimmed back, phrases which are not directly relevant have to be discarded. This has a very practical advantage: when you're speaking to people at five to seven and five to eight in the morning, between a farming report and the weather forecast, they don't need anything which might distract them from the basic message.

Another parallel to poetry is that the message is best expressed, not just in words of wisdom or of good advice, but in image and story. I have always found that I can communicate best what has been real in my own life – like the moment during my father's funeral which I shared in 'We Need a Fourth' – or the images and memories from my childhood in South Derry: the railway, the big snow of 1947, the Rocktown Road, or cutting turf in Ballinahone Moss.

Those childhood images have a power which goes far beyond the physical landscape. Ballinahone Moss is a lowland peat bog, heavily waterlogged with the rain flowing down from Slieve Gallon and the Sperrins. It needed constant drainage, and in spite of that you could feel the turf bank and the spreadground sway under your feet, as if it was precariously balanced on a lake of dark water. In some recess of the mind it was an image of threat and foreboding, and in August 1969 it became for me an image of political insecurity, while the then Prime Minister at Stormont, James Chichester Clark, struggled to hold together a disintegrating society:

> The moss sits on water
> in Ballinahone
> and spreadground for fresh cut turf
> is scarce.

But heathery scras*
pared from the bank
settle in wet grass
and bog cotton,
knit and bake
and make a shaky bottom.
The spreadground dries
with the turf.
Let Ulster pare heathery scras
for Clark,
before the water rises.

('Paring the Bank', August 16th, 1969)

scraith – Irish for a sod of topsoil, with roots of grass and heather

Not all the images and storylines come from my rural childhood. Pieces like 'Is it about a Bicycle?', 'Schindler's List' and 'Unfinished Work' flow from an interest in literature, cinema and early Irish art. Some, naturally, reflect the seasons of the Church's year, like Lent and Easter. There are echoes of the spirituality of Charles de Foucauld and of the Focolare.

Other stories and images came from my work and the travel which it sometimes involved: the

Vietnam Vets' Memorial in Washington DC, for example, and images from Rwanda after the massacres of 1994. Other reflections were inspired by people: family and friends and significant characters, like Jim O'Sullivan in Derry, Liam Miller of the Dolmen Press, my father's cousin Frank in New Brunswick, Jim Bradley of Strabane and even Pope John XXIII.

Writing requires either mighty will-power or strict deadlines. I am grateful to Jim Skelly, God rest him, to Bert Tosh, Martin O'Brien and all the people at the BBC who patiently pursued me year after year to keep the deadlines, and get up early, summer or winter, to speak the few words from the studios of Radio Foyle. And I am grateful to all at Veritas who gave me a new set of deadlines and took the risk of translating radio reflections into the printed word.

I síth agus i muintearas Íosa.

Oliver Crilly,
Ardmore, Co. Derry
August 2003

Acknowledgements

The talks which are reproduced here in printed form were originally written for radio. Talks 1–40 were broadcast on *Thought for the Day* on BBC Radio Foyle and Radio Ulster between 1982 and 2003. Talks 41: (i)–(v), titled 'Rwanda Sequence', were broadcast on *Prayer for the Day* – BBC Radio Four – in the spring of 2003. The author and publishers are grateful to the BBC for their co-operation.

Is it about a Bicycle?

There's a plaque on a house front in the Bowling Green in Strabane which marks the home of the writer Brian O'Nolan, or Flann O'Brien. In O'Brien's very funny book *The Third Policeman*, the desk sergeant in the police station greets every enquirer with the same question: 'Is it about a bicycle?' In the age we live in there is something innocent and refreshing about the sergeant's assumption that crime statistics exclusively consist of no lights, bad brakes, and at worst loose handlebars.

At the beginning of Lent in 1995, I was infected with the same insanity as Flann O'Brien's policeman. If Lent was not about a bicycle, at least there were several cycling memories which seemed to be related to Lent. The previous July, as we cycled in France, my brother Pat and I came across an article in a French magazine entitled *La Sagesse de la Bicyclette* – the wisdom of the bicycle. This wisdom, said the article, has to do with the combination of solitude and movement. Aha, says I to myself: Lent involves time for prayer and reflection, but also movement – a bit of progress. We're making an effort, and hopefully we should be going somewhere.

A more painful memory from that summer of 1994 was of the time I spent with a Trócaire delegation in Rwanda. Was it about a bicycle, you may ask? Strange as it may seem, in the midst of the hunger and disease and the refugee camps on the hills, there were a lot of bicycles. The day after we arrived in Cyanika, where the Medical Missionary sisters had their clinic, we went to visit the nearest camp, where several thousand people had erected little temporary huts of twigs and leaves. There at the foot of the hill a man was repairing an upturned bicycle – a solid machine with a well sprung saddle and rod brakes, and a very large carrier, a metal structure extended by the addition of wooden planks.

All the bicycles we saw had large carriers, suitable not only for a bag of rice or beans when they could be got, but also for carrying items of furniture during the long journeying of the displaced. We saw bikes with tables and chairs, and in one case even a complete iron bedstead, tied to the carrier. The overloaded bicycle almost symbolised the awful situation of war and famine and displacement. Lent reminds us of human situations we would rather forget. It should also remind us that we don't just fast for ourselves, but to share with the hungry and the anguished.

Lent is difficult. But then life is not all downhill either. There are times when we all need support. When the pressure's on, the solitude of the bicycle needs to yield to teamwork. The secret is not to go it alone: Christianity is about sharing the effort. Lord, be with me on the road; help me to keep pedalling, and give me the sense to let you control the handlebars.

The Lure of the Hills

I was born and reared in the foothills of the Sperrin mountains in the North-west of Ireland. From my home in County Derry we could look in one direction across Lough Neagh to the mountains of Mourne, and in the other direction towards our favourite local hill, Slieve Gallon. I have happy memories of Sunday afternoons in summer when we set out on bicycles to explore the slopes of Slieve Gallon, walking some of the steeper hills on the way up and enjoying the exhilaration of the downhill swoops with the wind in our faces on the way back.

In the summer of 1994 my brother and I reclaimed some of those early memories when we went on a cycling holiday in France. We explored the beauty of Burgundy on two sturdy mountain bikes, heading up into the hills by quiet country roads through fields of wheat and sunflowers and many little vineyards. The very first winding hill took us up from the river Yonne into the mountain village of Irancy, where a friendly countrywoman invited us into the little cellar which was the focus of the family's winemaking business for seven generations. We heard the gurgling of the vats where the last season's vine crop was working in the darkness as the next season's was ripening for the harvest.

After a week among the gentle hills and vineyards of Burgundy, we left the bicycles behind and took a train south to Toulouse. We still felt the lure of the hills, and early one morning we took a little train up into the Pyrenees as far as Lourdes. As the train pulled into the station, we saw a crowd gathered along the street, and we realised that they had come to see the start of a stage in the Tour de France cycle race. Fresh from the mountain bikes of Burgundy, we couldn't resist joining the crowd, and we had the pleasure of seeing some of the world's great cyclists, including the eventual winner of that year's Tour, Miguel Indurain, pedalling easily up the hill to the starting point.

Afterwards, we went down to the grotto of our Lady in Lourdes, a centre of faith and healing, thronged with pilgrims, including the crippled and the sick. The contrast was stark. We had just seen some of the world's strongest athletes at the peak of their fitness setting out to cycle up the great hills of the Pyrenees, and here were some of the world's weakest and most infirm. I saw a child on a stretcher whose hand had to be moved by the nurse as they approached the grotto. It's not that we had to deny the energy and the joy of the cyclists in their physical achievement in order to appreciate the suffering of the invalids. But we had to struggle to accommodate the two extremes of human experience, and to recognise the presence of the same God of power and compassion in the strength and in the weakness.

In the Hill Country of Rwanda

In August 1994 I visited Rwanda. From Nairobi we flew into Burundi and spent the night in Bujumbura. The following day we travelled by road through the hills into the South-west of Rwanda. The hills were steep and densely forested: great, dramatically beautiful mountains. Later, when we had arrived in the Gikongoro area, the hills were not so large and not so forested. The red earth was visible and many of the hills had camps of refugees or displaced persons living in little temporary huts of branches and leaves. We saw even more of the little huts when we arrived in Cyanika to visit the clinic which was being run by the Medical Missionaries of Mary.

Thousands of people were gathered in the area, and the Sisters treated about twelve hundred in the clinic every day. During the few days we spent there we visited the camps, and we prayed with the Sisters and listened to the story of their experiences, and the many stories of the pain and the courage of the Rwandan people among whom they lived.

Sister Josephine, who was looking after the pre-natal programme, told us about a young Rwandan couple who had arrived at the clinic just the day before we came. They had walked from Butare, a town about 25 kilometres from Cyanika which had been in the front line of the conflict. The wife was pregnant, and near her time for giving birth. Sister Josephine examined her and settled her in the clinic, and left her assistant to keep an eye on the young woman while she went down to the house.

The baby came sooner than expected, and Sr Josephine was called and went back up to the clinic. The child had been safely delivered, and the mother was resting on the floor of the clinic, on the only available blanket, which was an old blue plastic raincoat. She was holding her child on her shoulder. To Sr Josephine, she was like an image of our Lady in Bethlehem, a displaced person – an exile in her own country – giving birth to her child without home or comfort, without hope or prospects, among the steep hillsides where 600,000 people had found a precarious stopover between the massacres and the September rains.

In the anguish of that birth there is something of the tragedy of human life, just as, in the story of Mary, the anguish of the cross on the hill of Calvary was already mysteriously present at the manger on the little hill of Bethlehem. It's a long way from the sentiment of the plaster image we often see of Mary. And yet, out of the earthy realism of that birthplace, something flowers, as the glory of Mary flowered out of the suffering she shared with her Son and with Joseph.

Marbh le Tae agus Marbh Gan É*

I had been transferred from Melmount, Strabane, in the clergy changes of September 1999, and it was my first morning in Ardmore. After Mass, Geraldine and Deirdre, encouraged by Sr Teresa, came and offered to 'make the priest a cup of tea'. I explained that I had a tea caddy, but it was packed away somewhere in a cardboard box. However, I was able to produce a bag of tea, which I opened. I also produced a teapot and a spoon. My two visitors looked at each other. Then one said to the other: 'You're looking for *tea bags,* aren't you?' The other agreed.

I went through the ritual of warming the pot by rinsing it with boiling water, putting in the

* 'Can't survive with tea, and can't survive without it'

spoonfuls of tea leaves, boiling up the kettle again, pouring the boiling water over the tea leaves, and giving the teapot a plump on one ring of the cooker before pouring the tea for all of us. The ladies, by allowing me to make the tea, had succeeded in making me feel welcome and useful.

A couple of days later I had the opposite experience. Martin came to check out my computer, and when I offered him a cup of tea, he said: 'Marvellous – I love real tea', and he drank it black with neither milk nor sugar: clearly a real connoisseur.

The reference to 'real tea' took me back to the only time I ever saw real tea growing. I was on the way to Rwanda in 1994 with a Trócaire delegation. After flying into Bujumbura, capital of Burundi, we were travelling by road through the high mountains into south-west Rwanda. As we came around the great mountain passes, we caught glimpses of a green crop again and again down in the valleys. It was tea. It was ready for a harvest that would never come. No-one was left to harvest the tea or see to the process of marketing and distribution. I felt sad. I could remember the wet summer when it rained without stopping until the handcocks of hay rotted black in the wee field behind the house at home and my father felt hurt and helpless.

A lost harvest is a sad thing, but behind the ripening tea trees of Rwanda loomed the spectre of lost lives in war and massacre. In human experience lost life is the ultimate sadness, whether in Rwanda, in Kosovo, in East Timor, or in Northern Ireland. So often we look on helplessly after the event. But at least we should make a firm commitment that we will never consciously do anything that might put human life at risk. May God protect you, wherever you go.

Another Slunk

Towards the end of 1996, John Dunlop, Peter North and myself, with some of our back-up team, were travelling around Northern Ireland in a fascinating process of education and personal development as we worked on the Independent Review of Parades and Marches. On our way to Bellaghy, the back wheel of the Northmobile dropped into a hollow in the road. I explained to Peter North that many country roads around South Derry ran over what had been mossy ground. Under the road there had been soft peat, with occasional fir blocks, or lumps of bog oak. No matter how often the road was resurfaced, it tended to settle into a repeating pattern of hump and hollow. When a hollow was particularly deep, like the one we had just dropped into, we called it a slunk.

A day or two later we were driving on a mountain road into Pomeroy. The vehicle lurched as a back wheel once again dropped into a hollow on the side of the road. Without a moment's hesitation Peter North said: 'There's another slunk'.

The phrase came back to me at the beginning of 1998. The peace process had hit a few slunks. Like a moss road, the path of peace hides manys a fir block under the surface and manys a wet peaty hollow.

I remember my father telling stories of drawing turf out of Ballinahone with a horse and cart. Sometimes when a cartwheel dropped into a slunk, the load of turf would disintegrate and fall off. That didn't mean the job was abandoned. The cart had to be steadied, the horse quietened, and the load rebuilt, so that the winter's firing was got home.

Things could be worse. There were a few occasions when the moss road collapsed altogether, and horse and cart, collar and hems and britchin' all ended up in a deep moss hole.

The horse had to be loosed, and cart and wheels had to be taken apart, lifted out and reassembled on the road, before the turf could be picked up one by one and rebuilt for the journey home. Two things are worth noting: one is the perseverance involved; the other is the fact that all the neighbours, irrespective of creed or class, left their own turf bank and came with genuine enthusiasm to pull out the neighbour who was in difficulty.

At one stage in the peace process we had the Mitchell Principles. When we met Mo Mowlam to discuss Parades and Marches, I was tempted to suggest that she get the various protagonists to sign up to the Ballinahone Principles.

'We Need A Fourth'

On the day of my father's funeral in January 1997, I remember our last moment of farewell in the house before the lid was placed on the coffin. I remember friends and neighbours gathered outside the house, in the space defined by the garden wall and the outbuildings which my father had built with his own hands.

As the hearse moved slowly out into the lane – the loanin', we always called it – my two brothers, Tony and Pat, my nephew Paul and I carried the coffin for the first part of the journey. I remembered carrying my mother's coffin nearly eighteen years before on this same spot, and how the sharp edge of the wood cutting into my shoulder had in a strange way given me comfort. Cousins and neighbours carried my father's coffin in turn, and we walked behind them down the lane, between the whin covered rock and Willie John's field.

Just as we reached the turn in the loanin' before the final few yards to the county road, I felt a tap on my shoulder; it was Andy Kane. My father and Andy had a very special friendship for many years – which centred on Ballinahone Moss, where they both had cut turf in the time honoured way with the turfspade and with consummate skill. When my father had grown too old to cut his own turf, he insisted on getting his turf from Andy – real turf, not those machine turf which owed nothing to the skills of cutting and handling which had been passed on from generation to generation.

Andy had been a faithful friend, and even though his top quality turf were much in demand, he kept a few tractor loads every year, so that my father had good Ballinahone turf, and peace of mind about the winter's fuel, to the day he died. The fact that my father was a Catholic and Andy was a Protestant only served to underline the quality of their friendship.

What happened at the turn of the lane was totally unscripted, and totally appropriate. When Andy Kane tapped me on the shoulder, all he said was: 'There's three of us – we need a fourth'. Not only had Andy come to attend the funeral of his old friend, but he was indicating in unmistakable terms a sense of kinship with my father as a neighbour and as a fellow farmer and turfcutter, and he was paying a public tribute to a man with whom he had shared a mutual respect and trust.

Henry Scullion stepped over and joined the other three. As my father's coffin was carried the last few yards out on to the road, there were two Protestants supporting it on one side and two Catholics on the other, and they had linked their arms across each other's shoulders. I glanced at my brothers. We knew my father would have loved it.

Unfinished Work

I remember a rare good day towards the end of July 2002. I was returning from a few days Retreat with Fr Gerry Reynolds and a few friends near Navan in County Meath. On the way home I spent a few hours in Kells, which has a Derry connection, because of the Columban monastery. It is famous for the great illuminated manuscript, the Book of Kells. But the heritage of the monastery also includes a number of stone Scripture crosses.

I visited the Heritage Centre, and then walked up through the town to the site of the monastery, marked by the remains of a round tower. Just beside the tower is the oldest of the Kells crosses, the Cross of Sts Patrick and Columba, beautifully proportioned and covered with intricate carvings.

I stood for a long time, examining the various panels. Two Canadian tourists were walking around, and I showed them the image of King David, with what must be one of the oldest representations of a harp in the Irish visual tradition.

Then I walked over to one of the most fascinating of all the crosses – of special interest because it is unfinished. The geometry of the cross and the mass of the huge stone struck me powerfully. The heavy shaft of the cross had been chiselled away to leave a rectangle in low relief and two squares in deeper relief, ready for the carving of figures of different depth and emphasis. The ringed head of the cross was broken off at the top, but the carving of the Crucifixion at the centre stood out in bold relief, emphasised by the strong shadow cast by the summer sun. It showed the glorified Christ on the cross from the Gospel of John, with the sponge and the spear, the undivided garment, and the arms of Christ reaching out in welcome to the world.

The image of the unfinished cross came back to me on an autumn Sunday morning as I listened to a discussion on BBC Radio Ulster's *Sunday Sequence* programme about the *Power to Change* campaign. *Power to Change* was the brainchild of some Christian businessmen, who decided to use the power of the media to present the Christian faith. The idea was to catch the attention, and then to allow people to follow it up in their own way. It was designed as unfinished business. The Columban monks of Kells didn't plan an unfinished cross. But the unfinished cross is not a disaster. As the modern businessmen used the medium of advertising, the monastic artists used the medium of stone to create a striking profile for the figure of Jesus. How we finish the picture, and how we respond to Jesus on the cross, depends on us.

Vietnam Vets' Memorial

In May 1990 I went on a speaking tour in the United States with the Reverend Margaret Johnston, a Presbyterian Minister. The second stop on the tour was Washington D.C. On the Sunday morning we preached a shared homily in the New York Avenue Presbyterian Church, where Abraham Lincoln's pew is still in use. That afternoon, Scott and Beth McConnell, the young Presbyterian couple with whom I was staying, took me on a tour of famous sites in Washington, including the Washington and Jefferson monuments and the Abraham Lincoln Memorial. These were familiar images, but the one which was most unusual to me was the Vietnam Veterans' Memorial.

The memorial consists of a slice cut through a grassy hillside, faced with a wall of polished black

marble, like the marble of a shiny headstone.
Inscribed in the marble, from one end of the long
wall to the other, are the names of the Vietnam
dead, starting, where the wall is low, with the
smaller number of names from the beginning of
the war, while the highest part of the wall, at the
centre of the little hill, is crowded with the many
names from the height of the war, and then names
and hill both decline where the latter years of the
war are represented.

To appreciate the impact of the memorial you have
to walk along the paved area right beside the wall
in the company of the many people who still walk
it constantly, searching for the name of a loved one,
or rubbing an impression of the name on to a piece
of paper with a lead pencil. As the crowd moves
along, their coloured clothing is reflected in the
shiny marble, so that the names of the dead seem
to be suspended between two worlds of moving
figures and real and reflected landscape.

I came to see this place with the idea that it was a
memorial for something that was over. I think what
hit me hardest was that whatever was being
expressed here, it was clearly not over. I saw a girl

who couldn't have been more than twenty, with her mother and other members of her family, picking out a name and dissolving in tears. I saw the concentration on the faces, and the persistent pain of loss.

The following year, as I listened to the news reports of the Gulf war, that image haunted me. It is hard to think clearly about something which is so horrific and so immense that it practically takes over the total daily schedule of broadcasting. Utterly conflicting arguments seem to have some basis of truth to recommend them. Feelings are confused.

Many people were praying with great sincerity that war could be avoided. But war came. Where does that leave us? Where does it leave our prayers? One thing I am certain of: prayer is not less necessary in the event of war; when war begins – anywhere – it is even more important to pray that the world will be restored to sanity and peace.

In The Bunker

If you were in an air-raid shelter during massive bombardment by powerful hostile forces, do you think your favourite reading would be Jesus Christ saying: 'Love one another as I have loved you'? I think it would be pretty difficult to focus on the message of love in those circumstances, when all the human instincts would be pushing you towards fear and the desire for revenge. Yet that is precisely what happened in the town of Trent in Northern Italy in 1943, during the Second World War.

Chiara Lubich and her companions were a group of girls in their late teens and early twenties. From what we know of them, they were not the kind of people who would have had much time for what their own country's leadership was up to. In fact they were not the kind of people who would have had much time for war in any shape or form. Yet the war had devastated their lives, wiping out boyfriends, homes, careers.

Crouching in the air-raid shelter for hours on end, they began to ask themselves what could have lasting value, what could the war not destroy? They began to read the Gospels with a new urgency, desperately questioning their inherited faith for answers to the anguish of their situation. The words of Jesus leaped out at them from the page. Perhaps because they were so drastically at odds with what they were experiencing, they had to think deeply about them. Either these words were just out of touch with reality and not worth the paper they were written on, or they were a challenge which could turn upside down the accepted values of a world at war.

There was only one way to find out. They decided to test the words of Jesus, not just by thinking about them, but by putting them into practice. They could then see for themselves. When they tried to live the command of Jesus:

'Love one another as I have loved you', they experienced a great joy in the midst of the destruction. People around them experienced the warmth of their joy and called them 'focolare' – the hearth. From the utter powerlessness of cowering in the bunker, they were transformed into witnesses of the love of Christ: visibly radiant. From wondering what could be done about the problems of the world, they learned to confront the world by renewing themselves.

I am reminded of the prayer Cardinal Suenens wrote 'for the year 2000': 'Lord, give us the grace to be renewed in the Spirit and in fire. Teach us to speak to the world in tongues of fire. Let us bring to an end this time of uncertainty where Christians are timid and mute, discussing anxiously problems of today, as in the past on the road from Jerusalem to Emmaus, without realising that the Master is risen and alive'.

Resonances of Mind and Spirit

Amateur drama in Ireland is associated with Lent. In an earlier age, the dance halls were closed during Lent, and drama filled the gap in the schedules of parish halls. There was an extra buzz in Derry in Lent 2002 because the festival of amateur drama was taking place in the new and very professional theatre at the Millennium Forum.

My own interest in drama goes back to my student days in Maynooth. I remember being a policeman in *Arsenic and Old Lace*, and an Anglican clergyman marooned on an island in *The Admirable Crichton*. I remember helping to paint the set for Brian Friel's *The Enemy Within*.

It wasn't until I came as a curate to Strabane in 1982, however, that I experienced the full impact of amateur drama. The main local group was The Lifford Players. I still remember the quality and integrity of their production of Brian Friel's *Translations*, and the excitement when they won the premier award at the All Ireland finals in Athlone.

It was Jim Bradley, a founder member of The Lifford Players, who taught me most about the significance and the value of amateur drama with its roots in the local community. My first lesson was that amateur drama didn't mean poor drama. My second lesson was that drama was not just make-believe. I struggled with this idea for a long time. I tried to understand why a person of Jim Bradley's intellect and integrity and concern for all that is good in the local community should spend so much time and dedication on what seemed to be just passing entertainment.

When I got to know Jim better, I began to appreciate how he saw drama. For him, drama was an opportunity to explore and communicate resonances of the mind and spirit. The actor taking part in a play was offering a living body and a living voice to amplify and transmit those resonances. To be part of the audience was to be offered the opportunity to reflect on the human condition by being drawn into the experience of the characters on the stage.

I don't see it as a paradox that the drama festival season should happen during Lent. In these weeks we prepare for the drama of Holy Week. The authors of the Gospels created a whole new literary form to communicate what had happened in the life and death of Jesus Christ. They drew on the experience of Greek drama, especially the great Greek tragedies, and the resonances of the poetry and prose of the Hebrew Scriptures, to draw us emotionally and spiritually into the ultimate drama, where Jesus is the one who offers his living body and living voice so that we can hear and experience the compassion of God.

The Call of the Irish

A few years ago I had the privilege of collaborating with Fr Pat Ahern of the Irish Folk Theatre, Siamsa Tíre, in writing a new hymn for St Patrick. We agreed that two elements of existing hymns should be avoided: the dismissal of early Irish spiritual sensibilities as totally evil, and the presentation of Patrick himself as a sweet green shamrock encrusted plaster saint.

The pre-Christian spirituality of a people who could build Newgrange as a monument to light conquering darkness and life conquering death must have lent itself to fulfilment in the person who is the Light of the world and the Resurrection and the Life. And surely the Patrick who could light the Easter fire on the hill of Slane within seven miles of Newgrange, and choose Armagh as his headquarters in a challenge to the heart of spiritual and political power in the Ireland of his time, was no sentimental plaster nonentity.

The hymn we were writing was in Irish, and the word we settled on to describe Patrick was *creagach* – rocky, or craggy. The theme of the hymn was that this Patrick left his mark, in a living tradition expressed in stone and parchment and in the vibrant faith of generations. Happily, we don't have to depend on our own imaginations for our awareness of the spiritual energy which powered this man. He left us his *Confession* and the *Letter to Coroticus*, and from them we can uncover a deeply personal portrait.

At the core of Patrick's life story are the three formative experiences of imprisonment, prayer and mission. At the age of sixteen Patrick was an alienated teenager who had lost all sense of God. It was as a slave on the cold and inhospitable slopes of Slemish that he found again the depths within his own being and began to be open to God in prayer by day and night. Then, and later after he had escaped from Ireland, he was prepared for the urgent invitation to his life's work which he described as the call of the Irish. His struggle to answer this call was a struggle with himself and with many obstacles put in his way by other people, including his best friend who hurt him deeply by revealing a sin of his past. That struggle, like the exposure to the winter winds of Slemish, tempered his character and strengthened the qualities of the leader who would leave his mark on Irish Christianity.

When we trace the steps of Patrick back through the centuries we discover a point of intriguing convergence. Patrick the Briton, captured by the marauding Irish and held like an early Brian Keenan in captivity, returned to Ireland to forge a bond between these neighbouring islands. More than any recent document – more than our common membership of the European Union – Patrick brings Christians of all traditions closer to one another, because, in a poetic reversal of the call of the Irish, he calls all of us closer to Christ.

Esther

I came in late one night into the parochial house in Strabane and flopped into the armchair beside the range in the kitchen. More from force of habit than anything else I switched on the TV. I knew right away it was up-market television from the colourful costumes and settings. The titles were rolling at the start of the film, and they weren't in English or Irish. By the time the main title occupied the whole screen I had figured it was Hebrew, and when I laboriously read the main title letter by letter from right to left, it said ESTHER.

The film was by a subversive film maker in Israel. It was gripping – a human story of oppression and hatred, of violence, anger and revenge. I watched it through, until about half two in the morning. It was based on the book of Esther in the Bible, and when I eventually went upstairs I sat on the edge of my bed and read the book of Esther from beginning to end. It confirmed my impression that the script of the film was close to the original book in the Bible: it was nearly word for word.

Wasn't that fascinating? – subversion in Israel in the late twentieth century, using as a script the words of the Book of Esther from the Old Testament! The Good Lord works in strange ways. Imagine using a television programme in the middle of the night to remind me that the Bible is a subversive document. It can be very subversive for ourselves if we read it and take it to heart; and I can't imagine a more suitably subversive document for Christians in Northern Ireland than the Book of Esther.

In the citadel of Susa, Haman, the enemy of the Jews, had risen to power and had arranged to have all the Jews exterminated. Then, through the efforts of Esther, who was Jewish, her kinsman Mordecai replaced Haman in the king's favour: Haman was hanged and the tables were turned.

History held its breath. Then, sadly, the Jews did exactly as their enemies would have done and slaughtered those opposed to them.

You can see how subversive this story would be in present day Israel. But wouldn't it be a real breakthrough if we fellow Christians in Ireland could take the message to heart? *Esther* is presented as the story of Jewish victory and revenge; but precisely because of that revenge it is really the story of an opportunity lost. That's why it is so poignant for us. *We* have the opportunity to make a solemn commitment that no matter what swings of the power pendulum take place, none of us will ever again dominate or oppress the other, either by political manipulation or by physical violence and killing.

Roundabouts

The Fureys and Davy Arthur sang in the Melmount Parish Centre one night in January 1990. I don't know if it was their accents, or the fact that Finbar Furey talked about Ballyfermot, but whatever the reason it brought back a whole flood of associations for me. When I was working in Dublin, I had lived in Ballyfermot for a year, and I could see the familiar places again as I listened to the music. One very clear image was the big roundabout outside the entrance to the church. I used to wonder whether they built the roundabout at the church or the church at the roundabout.

At that time the big roundabout at Ballyfermot was almost unique, but that is certainly no longer the case – have you noticed the extraordinary proliferation of roundabouts in recent years? There are surely too many for it just to be a physical feature, a trend in town planning: it must be rising up from some deeper recess of the contempory psyche. Perhaps it is a symbol of confusion, or a reaction against a society which seems to require a non-stop progression of decisions, many of which have already been made by other people and which simply lie in wait for us to enter into them like some tragic inheritance.

For a while I thought that the increase in the number of roundabouts was due to a competitive spirit, and that the purpose was to achieve bigger and better roundabouts for possible inclusion in the Guinness Book of Records. But that theory also has been overtaken by the facts. Size is no longer relevant, as roundabouts are located in every conceivable place – not just in gay profusion around towns like Coleraine, but in odd and unusual places like the bottom of Broad Street in Magherafelt and even in an almost impossible corner of the Bowling Green in Strabane, under the very eye of the law.

Knockloughrim in County Derry can probably claim some kind of priority in the long line of unusual roundabouts. Many years ago on a Christmas morning the local people on their way to church, chapel or meetin' were confronted by an enigma. Some youths out late on Christmas Eve had stolen from the big house nearby the owner Sam's little wooden outdoor closet, itself almost as great a rarity in the area at the time as the roundabout, though Sam, the owner, called it 'the wee necessary'. The young men had set up the closet in the very centre of the crossroads, so that all the traffic had to veer around it. In the light of subsequent history it must be said that theirs was the first and original attack on the institution of the crossroads.

Perhaps it is time for someone to make a stand before the roundabout has finally overwhelmed all that remains of democracy. The good old crossroads stands firmly as a symbol of the clear-cut decision: you either do or you don't; there's a left and a right and a centre, and it's up to you to make a choice. Christianity has always presented that kind of challenge. We should know where we're coming from and where we are going: 'Halt

at the crossroads, look well, and ask yourselves
which path it was that stood you in good stead
long ago. That path follow, and you shall find rest
for your souls' (Jer 6:16).

Caught!

I had driven the eighty miles from Belfast to Strabane one November night in 1996. When I got into the house and switched on the light in the hallway I saw a little mouse-brown thing on the floor. A young bat, I thought. Bats are a protected species, and I had learned to be careful of them. On the other hand, I had a vague memory of a news report about someone who was bitten by a bat and got rabies or something.

I took off my overcoat and hung it up, glancing over my shoulder occasionally: I was afraid the bat would fly away and hide before I could decide what to do about it. A bat that you can see is one thing; a bat which is somewhere in the house but invisible is more serious – I had visions of waking up during the night to find it crawling over my face. I came back and looked more closely at it. Did it move, or was it just what some political activists like to call the illusion of movement? I wasn't sure. I took squarin's. That's a term from playing marbles, recently brought back into favour in a poem by Seamus Heaney. It means that you move around in order to avoid any obstacles, while keeping the same distance from your intended target.

I viewed the mouse-brown object from all angles, and was no farther forward. In the process I think I rendered a fair imitation of the gentleman who in a television commercial a few years ago danced exotically round a pint of his favourite beverage – only in my case there was no audible sound-track: I executed the manoeuvre in solemn silence and with total concentration.

I decided I would have to lift the little creature and take a closer look. Then, if it was alive I would bring it outside the door and set it free. I still remembered the news item about the bite and the rabies. I went upstairs and found the suede gloves my brother and his wife once gave me for Christmas. I came back down and put on the gloves. With my hands suitably protected, I circled my prey, held my breath and swooped. I got it.

As soon as I touched it I realised it was an autumn leaf, out of its natural habitat and, in its wing-like shape and mouse-brown colour, very effectively masquerading as a bat, but nevertheless just a leaf. My anxieties about a little wild creature being loose in the house, and about bites and rabies, had been ill-founded. I had been confused and misled, but I had also been given an object lesson. Before we act on our fears we should remember that often they are not based on reality at all, but on perceptions which were created by those very same fears in the first place.

Charles de Foucauld

The 1st of December 1916 was a Friday. That year it was actually the First Friday of Advent. It was during the First World War. In Tamanrasset in Southern Algeria, in the Sahara Desert, Brother Charles of Jesus – the Vicomte Charles Eugène de Foucauld – was shot dead by a nervous young Touareg tribesman, one of a party who had raided Charles' dwelling.

Charles had been born in Strasbourg in 1858, and had been an officer in the French army. He had lost his faith and had been living such a dissolute life that he had been thrown out of the army. Then he experienced conversion, and was as wholehearted in his acceptance of Christianity as he had been previously in his pursuit of selfish pleasure. He wrote to an army friend: 'As soon as

I believed there was a God, I saw that the only course open to me was to devote myself entirely to Him'.

After seven years in a Trappist monastery in Syria, he spent three years in the Holy Land, at Nazareth and Jerusalem, before setting out to live a solitary life among the Touareg in the Sahara Desert. His vision was to imitate Jesus and be a *'frère universel'* – a brother to everyone. He hoped that one day others would join him to live in small groups or fraternities among the poor and marginalised. This eventually happened, but not until some years after his death.

There are certain key words in the spiritual legacy of Charles de Foucauld. 'Desert', not surprisingly, is one, but it's not just a reference to the sands of the Sahara. Charles' desert is more like the *'díseart'* of the Irish spiritual tradition, which we get in names like Desertowen or Desertmartin. It means a remote place – desert, mountain or seashore – where we can experience the presence of God without distraction. 'Nazareth' is another key word. It refers to simplicity of lifestyle. Nazareth is a place where the word of God is conceived and nourished. It's not easy to find in our world, in December, in the mouth of a commercial Christmas.

The Muslim community celebrate Ramadan at that time of the year. It is good to remember the significant part played in Charles de Foucauld's conversion by his 'brothers of Islam'. Charles was amazed, as a French soldier in Algeria, to see the Arab soldiers take time for their prayers, even at the risk of being killed. He never forgot it. That level of commitment challenged him to find God again in his own life. And it gave a real impetus to his desire to be a universal brother.

Bread

Willie Peoples used to have his own uniquely personal way of indicating the days of the week. Monday and Tuesday were as you might expect them to be, but then Wednesday was 'Tuesday-go-by', and Thursday was 'Magherafelt Day'. It's a long time since I remember Willie among a squad of men gathering potatoes in the plantin' field, but Thursday is still Magherafelt Day for me.

One Thursday I was in Magherafelt, doing a bit of shopping for my father and myself. I came out of J.C. Stewart's and put the shopping in the boot of the car. I thought the oranges might run around in the boot, so I took them and a bottle of a well-known brand of sparkling spring water, intending to put them on the back seat. However, as I turned to unlock the door, one of the oranges ran away, and ended up under the next car. While I was bending down, awkwardly trying to see where it was, a kind lady sent her little son over to retrieve it for me.

She proved to be one of a number of fairy godmothers who were sent to be kind to this wandering scholar during the Magherafelt Day rounds. After a brief visit to Newsmarket in Rainey Street, I went up to McErlain's in the shopping centre, in search of bread. The little shop was full of women and children. The lady nearest me smiled and said: 'Blessed are you among women'. 'No,' I said, 'I think it's more like 'Give us this day our daily bread'.

She insisted on moving me past her in the queue, in spite of my best efforts to be courteous. When it came to my turn, I said to the girl behind the counter: 'Give me a big crusty, and two of the big round granary loaves, and two of these wheaten sides'. I got two bulging plastic bags, and I said: 'That'll keep me chewing till night'. The lady who had let me in front of her in the queue said: 'I'd sooner keep you a week as a fortnight!' I don't know what she'd have said if she'd seen me coming back later for the soda farls I forgot.

In a world filled with news of war and atrocity, the whole experience lifted my spirits. There was a wholesomeness and a warmth about it all. It reminded me of a saying of an American priest friend: 'The odour of sanctity is the smell of freshly baked bread'. I thought it was appropriate too that I had found such good humour and kindness on my shopping rounds during Easter week, when we are searching for signs of the Risen Christ among his people.

One of my favourite Gospel stories, and one that occurs in the liturgy of Easter week every year, is the story of the disciples on the road to Emmaus: how they walked in the company of Jesus, anonst* to themselves, and how they recognised him in the breaking of the bread.

* *unknown*

The Windmill Stump

I used to travel home from Strabane to visit my father every week. It wasn't just a journey in space from County Tyrone over the Sperrins into County Derry. It was like a journey in time as well, full of family associations. When I came down off the Glenshane Pass, or over the Hawe Brae from Tobermore, I turned left after Knockloughrim Station where my mother grew up, and then after passing through Knockloughrim crossroads I turned left again after the windmill stump.

The windmill stump is a major local landmark, and it's a family landmark too, because my father's grandfather, Mick Crilly, was at the building of it. We still have the mason's trowel he used in the work. I was delighted when the local

Methodist congregation built their new church and hall on the site, and I was delighted when the Reverend Fred Munce rang me to say they hoped to restore the old windmill.

Fred gave me a new perception of what restoring the windmill stump might mean. When it was talked about before, I thought of the external appearance of the windmill: restoring the black stone and red brick to its original strength and appearance. I thought of its impact on the landscape at the new church: a unique round tower on a site like an early Irish monastery. I thought of its continuity, bringing the craftsmanship of Mick Crilly and his colleagues fresh into a new century and a new millennium.

Fred didn't contradict any of that, but he added something else. I had been thinking of the space outside the building. He brought me inside the windmill. He spoke of renewing the wooden beams and floors. He spoke of a room where people could meet: not just a room for the Methodist congregation, but a gathering place open to all the local community.

What he said made a lot of sense to me. On my next journey over the Sperrins I thought deeply about it. So often we limit ourselves and our energies to preserving the external appearances. We're great monument people; the people of the stone. In our politics we have a total and uncompromising commitment to *our* version of the institution, *our* windmill of black stone and red brick. It doesn't much matter if it's like the windmill stump in Knockloughrim, which hasn't had sails or working parts in our lifetime. We'd sacrifice our own and others' lives for it.

Fred's vision makes more sense. It's the inside of our windmill that counts. We'll honour the hands that built the windmill when we create in it a space where we can make room for one another, where we can invite one another into our lives and into our institutions. Jesus said: *Love one another*, and even: *Love your enemies*. It doesn't come easy – we have to want it and we have to work at it. But it can be done. You should see the size of the wee mason's trowel that was used to build the windmill in Knockloughrim.

The Runaway Train

The road drops so steeply off the Glenshane Pass down to Maghera that you'd swear you were on perfectly flat ground from Maghera to Knockloughrim. But you'd be mistaken, as anyone who ever rode a bicycle down the old road could tell you. You didn't need to pedal to reach breakneck speed down the hill. There was a steep gradient on the railway, too. When the big excursion trains left Magherafelt for Coleraine, they needed a second engine to cope with what was referred to as the Maghera Bank, the hill that faced them as they moved out of Knockloughrim Station, under the Derganagh bridge.

About 1929, a large section of goods train made the downhill journey without the aid of any engine. On the way from Magherafelt to

Coleraine, it was shunting at Maghera station, leaving some wagons off and taking on some more. A young visitor at the station released the brake on the Guard's Van at the Knockloughrim end, and a few yards took the van and thirteen wagons out of the station and on to the Maghera Bank. The young lad was helpless in the van, and the porter who had been working at the shunting linked the shunting pole under one of the wagons and sat on it, holding on to the side of the wagon. The runaway train gathered speed, lurching towards Knockloughrim.

My two uncles at Knockloughrim station, which was their home, heard the train approaching and ran out to look. As it came round the bend and under the bridge, the Maghera porter was on the same side as the platform, and would have been crushed. He jumped just in time. My uncle James was quick on his feet; he ran along the platform as the train slowed a little, and dropped the hand brake on the side of every second wagon. The brakes couldn't be secured, but it was enough, and the runaway ground to a halt in Crilly's cutting.

Now there was a whole new problem: how to shift a train which officially didn't exist. The runaway train had managed to insert itself into a section of single track without clearance. A metal tablet had normally to be exchanged, and only the train which had the tablet was authorised to enter the section of line. In terms of bureaucracy, the train in Crillys' cutting wasn't there at all. It took a whole new shunting of systems before an engine could be got back down from Maghera to clear the line.

The Derry Central railway may be gone, but nothing changes. Part of the problem of our society is related to momentum: when something has been building up a head of steam for twenty years, or even for centuries, it takes more than the flick of a hand brake to slow it down; and if the line is ever to be cleared, we will have to recognise that reality is more important than bureaucracy or ideology.

Flags

On the eleventh and twelfth of July 1998, my brother Pat and I booked in with Irish Cycling Safaris for their Tour de France weekend. All went well and not ill. We cycled out in a light drizzle on Saturday morning, struggled over the Hill of Howth, and returned in time for a light lunch. Then we headed for O'Connell Street to watch the Prologue Time Trial.

We found a vantage point right in front of the columns of the GPO, giving us a view all the way down to O'Connell Bridge, to where the cyclists came round the final corner off the quays and hit their full rhythm on the home straight. The spectators had caught the atmosphere of the Tour, and young lads heightened the excitement by pummelling the advertising panels on the barriers along the street as each cyclist came into view. The announcers gave us the names of the riders, a bit of information about them, and their time as they flashed past the finishing line. Their speed was emphasised by the way the accompanying cars had to rev to keep up with them.

There were 189 riders, and we stood for four hours and saw them all come in. The first few riders recorded a time of just over seven minutes. Then, as good time triallists came through, the time was whittled down towards the six minutes fifty, then forty, then into the thirties and the twenties. When the big names came, Alex Zulle and Jan Ullrich clocked six minutes nineteen, Laurent Jalabert and Bobby Julich reduced it to six minutes seventeen. Abraham Olano made six sixteen. But the day belonged to the British rider, Chris Boardman. He looked very fast as he came down O'Connell Street, and the crowd held their breath as the time was announced: six minutes twelve seconds. When he was confirmed the overall winner and first wearer of the Yellow Jersey in the Tour de France en Irlande, O'Connell Street erupted in celebration. A group of British supporters beside us, right in the centre of the GPO façade, unfurled a huge silky sparkling clean Union Jack, and it billowed up across the columns of the Dublin GPO, with all its history, and with its tricolour flying. The whole throng, international, European, British, and Irish of all persuasions, rose with the billowing flags in a unanimous acknowledgement of Chris Boardman's achievement. It was a wonderful moment, and a sign of hope: that we can rejoice together, and our flags can fly in friendship and not in confrontation.

Schindler's List

Schindler's List is a memorable film. There's the fine acting, including that of the Ballymena man, Liam Neeson. There's the impact of the black and white filming – like wartime newsreels – especially in the scene where the trainload of women pulls into the dark entrance of Auschwitz, and the big chimney stack belches clouds of ominous smoke into a heavy sky. And there's the reality of what the film is all about, because this is not some remote fictional horror, but part of the history of the peoples of Europe during my lifetime.

After I had seen the film, I was looking through the book on which the film was based: *Schindler's Ark*, by Tom Keneally. I was struck by the foreword in which Tom Keneally reflects on the difficulty of writing such a book. One of the great difficulties he mentions is that evil generally achieves a certain predictable and measurable success in works of popular fiction – and indeed in the kind of real life where a woman can be killed and dumped in a wheelie bin, and we are supposed to believe that the equally ruthless killing of an alleged killer will make it all right.

Against that background, a story which chronicles the pragmatic success of good over evil can appear a bit naive. There is an inevitability in the persistence of evil and in the power of evil which has given credibility to novels and to drama as far back as the great Greek tragedies, and which has persuaded even political idealists down the centuries that the way to success is to imitate the ruthlessness and cruelty of the tyrannies they oppose.

To believe in cold steel and bombs and bullets is to believe that to overcome the worst in human nature, one has to take on the worst in human nature. It's a sickeningly plausible lie, a lie which has been sold very effectively by the hard men of history, especially when they can justify it by claiming that, well, it mightn't usually be acceptable, but you know, there's a war on, and this is the reality of war.

I have heard reviewers of the film *Schindler's List* say that the film is justified by the fact that it provides a graphic reminder of the reality of the Holocaust: a reminder of the horror and reality of evil in the world. Reading Tom Keneally's foreword to *Schindler's Ark*, I came to the conclusion that both book and film are justified by the fact that they provide a graphic reminder of the persistence of good in human nature, even in a self-centred, sensual, scheming man like Oskar Schindler.

In this real life story, compassion grows in the most unlikely context, and overcomes greed and cold calculating evil. Like a fresh green shoot breaking through the icy soil of winter, love persists, and as Carl Jung once noted: *Where love rules, there is no will to power*, just compassion and the protection of the weak.

The Shadow of Bealnablath

One night I watched bits and pieces of a programme on television called *The Shadow of Bealnablath*. It was about the shooting of Michael Collins. Between doorbells and phonecalls I picked up snatches of the history of guerrilla warfare and Treaty negotiations and the emergence of Collins as the Commander in Chief of the forces of the new Irish Free State.

What intrigued me most, though, was not the story of the years of history, but a single moment, a split second of decision or of indecision before an IRA marksman pressed the trigger of a .303 rifle and Michael Collins fell fatally wounded at Bealnablath. The shadow of Bealnablath is the shadow of that moment, and it is a shadow which lies over us even now.

The mentality of that moment was the mentality that sees only a target. The horizon of the world is narrowed to that little concentrated circle which is viewed down the sights of a rifle. It is a perspective which is necessary for the business of killing. Without that narrow field of vision, how could you place a bomb in Sion Mills, for instance, without giving any thought to the old couple watching television in a darkened house, or the possibility of passers by on a main road, or the image of Christ and his apostles on the façade of the nearby church, symbolising values of compassion and concern for your neighbour?

The logic of that moment in Bealnablath was the inexorable logic of violence. It is not clear that even Michael Collins' enemies wanted him killed; certainly many who were on the other side in the Irish civil war lived to look back with regret at that killing. There is something approaching Greek tragedy in the piling up of coincidence upon seeming coincidence in the lead-up to the fatal ambush, and in the almost accidental death by violence of a man who had himself been driven to use violence in the hope that it might lead to something different. Surely the significant legacy of his experience is the understanding that it doesn't, that in fact it cannot?

If Greek tragedy is about inevitability, Irish tragedy is about brothers. The anti-Treaty Irishmen who ambushed Michael Collins had been his comrades. Two of the men involved on opposite sides on that day were quite literally brothers. We are in fact all brothers and sisters in Ireland: not just brothers and sisters within our own part of the community, but all of us – brothers and sisters because we share a common humanity, and believe it or not for the most part also a common Christianity, rooted in a common Baptism.

All tragedy is about decisions and where they lead. If you ask me why that split second at Bealnablath has remained with me to trouble my consciousness and to question my understanding, I think it is because it could have been different. It is of the essence of decisions that they can be different: a man does not have to shoot his brother.

Smoke

There was a fair bit of sunshine around in Strabane on the 25th of April 1993, once the morning mist lifted, but the landscape of the mind was dominated by smoke. The last trails of smoke over the Branch Davidian compound in Waco, Texas, had scarcely dispersed in the columns of our newspapers before they were filled with pictures and reports of London bombs and a booby-trapped car near Cookstown. The image of people fleeing for their lives in a London street, pursued by a billowing cloud of smoke and dust, evokes a lot of smoke-filled images – from the London blitz, from Belfast and Dublin, from Derry and Enniskillen and Warrington.

One thing is sure: people who detonate explosives as a method of creating social or political movement cannot any longer claim that they didn't foresee the consequences in lost lives and human anguish. Violence contains its own logic of devastation, whether it is let loose in London or in Castlerock or in Srebrenitsa. And like the smoke and the shrapnel, it does not confine its attention to one small discreet target area. Its effects are indiscriminate, and in the long term take their toll of those who initiate the violence just as much as of those who are the intended targets.

Where violence and hatred have been given their head, as in what once was Yugoslavia, the horror of the end result should surely stand as a grim warning to the rest of us. What we have experienced is bad enough. Only the grace of God and the goodness of countless nameless people who have chosen the way of patience and forgiveness have prevented the ultimate catastrophe, from which no-one would emerge victorious. It's certainly not that we're not capable of all that is worst in human nature. History tells us very clearly that no people is exempt from the instinct to dominate and destroy. Sin flows in our veins like the blood which can so easily be shed.

Whatever has held the line for us, bad and all as we are, needs to be cherished and encouraged. If we don't improve we may get worse. I think those of us who claim a Christian allegiance have a special responsibility to build on what is positive in our society, and to respond to what is good in each other's attitudes and traditions.

Whatever progress can be made, either at inter-church level, or in cross-community activities or in political structures, it all must begin with attitudes and personal commitment: at the level of the heart. The fifty days between Easter and Pentecost symbolise the forty-nine years plus one of Israel's Jubilee. The fiftieth year was the year of amnesty, when debts were cancelled and prisoners released, and there was universal forgiveness. Jesus drew on this evocative memory when he said we should forgive seventy times seven times: total amnesty multiplied by ten. It's hard, but then so is the smoke and the shrapnel. Was it Henry Kissinger who said: 'Nothing clarifies the mind like the absence of alternatives'?

News for the Poor?

I was born into a world at war in 1940. One day, after the war was over, among the whins and briers on a rocky height near Knockloughrim, we found a soldier's helmet, abandoned after manoeuvres towards the end of the war. We called it a tin hat. In spite of an early memory of soldiers shaving in cold water out of their upturned tin hats near our house on a winter morning, the tin hat spoke of a war that was totally remote from our childhood experience. Continuous television images of war in Iraq, even with a note on the screen saying the coverage is live, can seem strangely remote also.

But the effects of war are not remote. They are brutally real. Iraq is on a completely different scale from our own 'troubles', but we don't have to be told of the effects of bullets and bombs on human flesh. The anguish of war haunts the minds and hearts of suffering survivors for years afterwards, as the aftermath of massacre haunted the hotel-room I stayed in in Rwanda in August 1994, where I picked my steps by candlelight among the pools of congealed blood on the carpet.

Anti-war demonstrations around the world showed that opinions were divided on many issues around this war: about the decision to fight, about the political processes and the role of the UN, about the handling of humanitarian aid during and after the fighting.

When it is all over, many issues will remain. One in particular concerns the cost of the war: the human cost, the international political cost, and quite simply the financial cost. The forty Cruise missiles used on the first night of the war cost twenty-four million dollars. One stealth bomber costs four billion dollars – four thousand million – which could clear the entire debt of Zambia. President Bush asked for an additional seventy-five thousand million dollars in a supplementary budget for the war. When governments are really committed to something, money can always be found. If this kind of money were regularly committed to world development, how many of the world's problems could be solved without recourse to war?

Compassion is vital to solving the world's problems. Compassion is vital in our response to war in Iraq: compassion for the people of Iraq, compassion for soldiers caught up in it and for their families, especially for the families of the dead: a totally inclusive compassion, with no exceptions.

Rodin

I was at a meeting in Paris once, and I slipped off by myself for half a day to see the work of the sculptor, Auguste Rodin, at the Rodin Museum, a big old house with a garden in front and an even bigger garden at the rear.

When I arrived at the house, I went into the front garden. After walking around for a while, I stopped by a group of bronze figures called 'The Burghers of Calais'. The burghers were a group of the better-off citizens of Calais, who had been caught up in the horrors of a siege. The massive sculpture was commissioned in their memory.

I stood in front of the figures, trying to interpret their attitudes and their expressions. Then I noticed that Rodin had left an empty space at the edge of the group, and I stepped up close, as if I were part of the sculpture. It gave me a fresh angle on the whole thing. None of the figures was looking at me. There was a physical space for me, but I could not become part of the group. Then I realised that the figures weren't looking at each other either. The sculptor had locked each character into isolation. Here was a group of people in the closest proximity to one another, sharing a common plot of ground, sharing a common destiny, but unable, unwilling, to communicate with one another even by a glance. I was stunned.

I went through the house and out into the garden at the back. There was a long rectangular pool of water, and at the far end a sculpture which had been commissioned as a war memorial. It was a powerful evocation of combat, too sharply and painfully real for the people – another set of burghers, no doubt – who had originally commissioned it. As I walked up along the rectangular pool, a little brood of baby ducklings waddled out from behind the base of the statue and headed for the water. Can you imagine the contrast between the cold hard bronze, and what it expressed, and the little fluffy yellow creatures?

I retreated into the house, sympathising with the patrons who had been presented with a glimpse into the painful reality of war and killing, when all they wanted was something symmetrical and superficial.

Inside the house, I came across a bronze representation of two hands. My first reaction was to say 'Oh yes, praying hands', but then I got close enough to read the title. It said 'La Cathedràle' – 'The Cathedral'. I was puzzled. I walked around the plinth, looking at the hands. I walked around it two or three times. Eventually it struck me that the outside of the hands wasn't really holding my attention: my eyes were being drawn inside – to the palms of the hands, where the light was concentrated. Then I knew why it was called 'The Cathedral'. What Rodin had sculpted was not so much the hands as the space between the hands: it was sacred space – space where there was room to grow, room to be, room to give glory to God.

Risks

One of the sad and paradoxical things about late April and early May 1994 was the number of deaths that were reported in the world of sport. Boxer Bradley Stone died from brain injuries sustained during a fight. Irish jockey Declan Murphy was very seriously injured when his horse fell during a race at Haydock Park. Dr Alan Larkin died after he had collapsed during the Belfast marathon. Ayrton Senna, the Brazilian racing driver, died in a high speed crash in the San Marino Grand Prix. Austrian driver Roland Ratzenberger had already died in a similar crash during a qualifying lap.

Ayrton Senna's death in particular made a huge impact all over the world. It's not easy to forget the image of the car entering the corner and then taking off, not with a bump as if it had hit anything on the track, but in a continuous glide, like a stunt plane peeling off from formation – only to crash sickeningly into the wall beside the track. Brazil held three days of national mourning, and then gave him a funeral with a level of ceremony usually reserved for a head of state: his yellow helmet on the flower-strewn coffin, military style honours, and a large S written in white in the blue sky by airforce jets.

During the days when so many sporting tragedies were being reported, each day also saw headlines in our local papers telling of deaths by paramilitary violence: a man shot while watching television; two men shot while serving behind the counter, one of an angling shop, the other of his newsagent's and confectionery premises; another man shot as he walked to work accompanied by his wife. The list got longer every day.

Between the sporting deaths and the deaths from paramilitary violence there is a great chasm. Certainly, many may feel that boxing should be banned or more strictly controlled, that safety measures in motor sport should be tightened up.

But those taking part in sport are seeking success, and for that success are prepared to take great personal risk – even risk to their own lives. At what point that risk becomes too great to be acceptable is a matter for serious debate. However, it is a debate about risk and personal commitment, not about seeking death.

There is shock and anguish over the sporting deaths, but at the heart of the matter there is something which survives. There is a total commitment, a giving without counting the cost. Paramilitary killing has death as its object. It removes the option of life. It is the ultimate totalitarianism, attacking life itself. Nothing survives.

St Paul used the commitment of the athlete in training and competition as a symbol and a challenge for the sincere Christian. What risks are we prepared to take to bring an end to violent deaths, to bring about a society in which not only neighbours are loved, but even enemies are loved?

Church on a Plate

Dr John Dunlop and I had arrived at Aldergrove – Belfast International Airport – in the early morning, having flown in from Washington DC via London Heathrow. My case was delayed in London and I had to clear it through the customs in its absence. The customs man asked me to sign a form to acknowledge any dutiable goods.

The only thing of interest in the case was a plate: a good delph plate, but not the sort you're supposed to eat off. It was produced to mark the two hundredth anniversary of the First Presbyterian Church in Pittsburgh, and when we visited there, John and I were given one each by the Pastor, the Rev. Leslie Holmes. The church, built on land given by descendants of William

Penn, is pictured on the plate, and is a lovely reminder of our visit.

We took part in a service in the church, and John preached a very moving sermon. I was intrigued by the Scripture passage he chose: it was from John, chapter 5, about the paralysed man at the pool of Bethzatha. I had chosen a passage for another talk during our tour, and it was about a paralysed man also – the man who was let down through the roof by his friends at the very feet of Jesus in Mark, chapter 2. I thought it was interesting that we had both drawn on the image of a paralysed person for our reflection on our situation in Northern Ireland. Maybe it's not so strange, since we have been paralysed during years of conflict – paralysed by fear, by distrust, by prejudice, by bad experiences, by lies that we have told ourselves, by ideas that other people have instilled into us, and more recently by the effort to find a way forward.

John and I both started off by acknowledging the paralysis, admitting the real pain of our society. So many people have been killed, so many seriously wounded in body and spirit. But we were also searching, trying to bring faith to bear on the situation. Both stories from the gospel presented a paralysed person. Both stories also presented the healing power of Jesus. I have always been fascinated by the characters who carried their friend to Jesus and got up on the roof to lower him down to Jesus' feet. These were people of faith, but also people of courage, imagination and initiative. They believed that Jesus was in town and could help their friend.

That wintry day in Pittsburgh, John Dunlop challenged us to that kind of faith and courage also. He underlined the question of Jesus to the paralytic at the pool: 'Do you want to be well again?' As Christians we cannot settle for a paralysis that ties us to the past. We have to look together towards the future, believing in the presence and the power of Jesus.

The Gift of Tenderness

In April 1994 I attended a special Mass in
Faughanvale at which Bishop Edward Daly
confirmed ten handicapped young people: anointed
them with chrism and claimed their gifts for the
building up of the Church. When Bishop Daly
spoke to the young people about their value and
their gifts, I knew he wasn't just saying something
for the occasion: he meant every word of it. As the
week went on, and I listened to the news from
Gorazde and Johannesburg, from Garvagh and
Belfast, I realised more than ever how much we
need the gifts of our handicapped people.

The first gift which was very evident in
Faughanvale on Sunday afternoon was the gift of
tenderness. This church, which had throbbed with
the anguish of funerals after the 'Trick or Treat'

Halloween massacre at Greysteel, was vibrant now with the tenderness and affection of the handicapped and their families. I found the group from my own parish, and Veronica greeted me with a great hug – reminding me of the care of the first Veronica who wiped the blood and sweat from the face of Jesus. The young people were smiling as they greeted each other and their families and friends, and I was moved by the gentle care of the families for their special members.

There was also the gift of acceptance. Nobody was there to pass judgment on anyone else, to say: my situation is better or worse than yours. It reminded me of St Paul's advice: 'Make hospitality your special care'. The hospitality wasn't just about having room in the house or sharing food around the table. There was sharing, but most of all, people created space where everyone could feel welcome and appreciated. There was the celebration of Confirmation, and there was also the celebration of affirmation. As my mother, God rest her, used to say: 'It would've done your heart good'.

There was a gift of joy, as well. It is a deeply human and deeply Christian paradox that it is often people who have suffered greatly who have learned the meaning of true and lasting joy. Those who have suffered possess a precious gift. Jean Vanier, founder of the L'Arche communities for the mentally handicapped, writes: 'Do not run away from people who are in pain or who are broken, but walk towards them, to touch them. Then you will find rising up within you the well of love, springing from resurrection'.

In the anguish and joy of South Africa in those same weeks of 1994, it was good to see Nelson Mandela walking forward from a painful past of violence, suffering and imprisonment, and taking the path of reconciliation and reconstruction, while Bishop Edward Daly, who had himself experienced a great deal of pain over the previous twenty years, was saying to those on the path of violence: 'End the killing once and for all'. He added: 'Good will eventually prevail over evil. I have great hope for this community'. I felt great hope at the Confirmation in Faughanvale. I also wondered which of us really are the handicapped?

The Issue is the Relationship

The leadership of Worldwide Marriage Encounter had a great gift for creating memorable slogans. I think a lot of the credit for that must go to Fr Chuck Gallagher, a big-hearted American Jesuit. Chuck had the capacity to express himself in words which sounded cheeky and way out, but which had a core of wisdom and truth.

One of the slogans which has stayed with me over the years is 'Love is a decision'. It means that we should be good to one another, not just because we feel like it, or when we feel like it, but because it is the right thing to do, because whatever our mood of the moment we want to put each other first. That applies in the first instance to married couples, whose life commitment is to put each other first, but because the marriage relationship is such a strong symbol of relationship in general, it applies to relationships in the wider community also.

As well as 'Love is a decision', another slogan has always impressed me by its cheeky upside down logic. It says: 'The issue is not the issue; the issue is the relationship'. The starting point is that when a married couple are at war, the cause of the fighting, and the resolution of it, is to be sought, not in the item the argument appears to be about, but in what is hurting them in their relationship. When that is sorted out, the issue they think they're fighting about will seem much less important.

While it began as a slogan for married couples, 'The issue is the relationship' had certain overtones for the days when Senator George Mitchell was coming towards the end of his review of the Good Friday Agreement. The discussions were into extra time, and it was clearly not going to be easy. Once again it was a time for prayer: prayer not just that the issues might be resolved, but that the people who needed to resolve the issues might succeed in resolving the core issue of who they are to one another and who they want to be in a future that can be shared.

As the process developed, there were some indications that, as well as confronting issues, those engaged in the discussions were communicating at a personal level, which had not always been the case before. Communication is a sign of hope, and so, strangely, is the shared experience of pain. The suffering of recent years is not all waste: out of it can come a new strength and creativity. Fr Augustine Karakezi of Rwanda said of his people, both Hutu and Tutsi, after the massacres of 1994: 'They have suffered such experiences. If they are healed, we will have people of such quality'.

The Drama of Holy Week

The weeks leading up to Holy Week and Easter coincide with the season of the drama festivals. The story of the festivals is generally one of creativity and community building. Amateur drama is a cross-community activity, and helps us to cope with life either by laughing at ourselves or by reflecting on painful issues by seeing them at a distance in the story of someone else's life. Part of my enjoyment of a drama festival is that we not only see the play, but we hear the adjudication afterwards. The adjudicator's comments can make a good play seem even better, and – dare I say it – sometimes a bad play interesting.

Perhaps it's because of years of listening to adjudications that, when I come to think about Holy Week, I see it in terms of drama. First of all, there's drama in the setting. I once visited the Holy Land, and can remember standing on the Mount of Olives where Jesus wept over Jerusalem. What amazed me was how small the distances were. The dramatic effect was heightened by the fact that the steep drop into the gorge of the Kedron Valley was more impressive than the short distance across to the city walls.

When Jesus made his entry into Jerusalem on Palm Sunday, it wasn't a long march like those made by Mahatma Gandhi or Mao Dse Dung. It was more like a sabbath stroll. It was still quite dramatic. The intensity of the emotion surrounding such a journey is not in direct proportion to its length. When Jesus chose to make the journey on a donkey, it was a very dramatic way of proclaiming that he came in peace. There was joyful drama in the palm branches.

A few days later, when he journeyed down the Mount of Olives again by night into the Garden of Gethsemane, the drama was turning into something more like Greek tragedy, but it was not that Jesus was just passively accepting the inevitable. The Gethsemane experience is so deep and of an intensity so absolute that the rest of the journey becomes a calm, self-assured progression to the fulfilment of the Cross – especially in the Gospel of St Luke, where it is completed by Jesus' trusting abandonment to the Father: 'Into your hands I commend my spirit'.

It's a pity that so often our most intense and challenging experiences are thrust upon us, without much involvement or preparation on our part. It's not that we should over-dramatise our lives, or forsake the reality of the present to live in the future, but it might be good if we could face some of our challenges ahead of time. I can't remember who it was who said: 'If you wait till the end of your life to die, it will be too late'.

Whin Blossoms and Daffodils

I associate Eastertime with whin blossoms and daffodils. Whins grew thickly over the hill we called the rock, beside our house where we grew up, and as Easter approached they heaped bright yellow blossoms over dark green bushes all along the loanin' to the county road. My father, God rest him, added to this background a foreground of daffodils, more fresh green crowned with bright yellow. In case you're thinking of a few daffodils on the edge of a garden, my father grew so many daffodils that my cousin Mary was able one year to gather enough to provide a daffodil as a sign of hope for every person coming out of the nine o'clock Mass at the Milltown chapel in Magherafelt on Easter Sunday morning.

Whin bushes are prickly things – jaggy, we would have said – but in their own way they are also a symbol of hope. Whins are the oldest form of vegetation in this part of the world, apparently. They have flourished on the Sperrin mountains not just for thousands of years, but for millions of years. I find that an extraordinary thought: that in spite of the exposed landscape of places like the Glenshane Pass, in spite of snow and ice and prevailing winds, in spite of children who considered burning whins a delightful pastime long before joyriding was ever thought of, these prickly green bushes persisted tenaciously in the most inhospitable of landscapes, and faithfully put forth their bright yellow blossoms in the Spring of every year, spreading beacons of warmth and brightness in the darkness of receding wintry days.

We used to hardboil eggs in whin blossoms on Easter Monday, and roll the deep yellow eggs in one of the fields behind the house, in a ritual which probably went back to pagan times and had something to do with the persistence of life through the annual cycle of winter and spring. Whatever its origin, it matched the mood of Easter celebration. The bright yellow of daffodils and whin blossoms is a joyful colour, and a symbol of light conquering darkness and life conquering death. Each year, as we look forward to Easter, I thank God for the daffodils gradually unfolding, and for the yellow of the whin blossoms spreading and deepening over the landscape.

They're there for all to see, as the joy of Easter is for everyone, and they point to light and colour and life. They are like the premonition, beyond the Cross, of the glory of an Easter dawn.

The Big Snow

My uncle Dinny once consulted the doctor about some aches and pains. The doctor asked him: 'When did you last look at your birth certificate?' The comment came back to me on a winter's day as I was plouterin' round in the fresh snow while visiting the sick. I realised that I could remember the snowstorm of 1947. I remember my father, God rest him, making a path through the deep snow down the loanin' to the county road, and then along the road, over McKee's height, past the plantin' gap and Arrells' loanin', and down the Big Hill to the main road at Knockloughrim.

My father first lifted the fresh clean white top of the snow with rhythmic sweeps of the long handled shovel, as he would have mowed corn with rhythmic sweeps of the scythe, and then scobed the red rotten-rock surface of the loanin' itself to create a secure path underfoot. The red gravelly marks of the shovel left a pattern all the way along the piled snow. I was not quite seven years old, and not very tall. It's no wonder it is one of my earliest memories. If I had been able to express it in Biblical terms, it was an Exodus experience, like an Israelite walking a precarious hewn path through a red-flecked sea of white.

When my father talked of the Big Snow of 1947, he would recall a neighbour's funeral, where the coffin had to be carried across the open field to the road, because the drifted snow had completely closed the loanin' which was the normal access to the farmhouse. The snow in our loanin' was deep to begin with, and when piled up on either side to clear the path, it was far above my head, and I couldn't see over it.

The image has lurked in my memory as a symbol of tunnel vision and lost perspectives. Now, looking back over the years, I reflect that a community, like a snowbound child, can be cut off from a wider vision of reality. But I take comfort from the fact that after the Big Snow came the thaw, and a belated spring, and I could see around me as the white world yielded to the bright yellow of the daffodils and the whin blossoms. When progress in our society seems slow and uncertain, we need to be reassured that spring will yet come. The walls of frozen prejudice and hatred can eventually melt, like the snows of '47, and a community, like a child, can grow up to the full vision of a landscape of hope.

Like Little Children

I often wondered what exactly Jesus meant when he said: 'Unless you change and become like little children'. He couldn't have meant the limiting things, like not being able to reach up to the table, or not being able to see beyond the horizon of their own little world. I have been taking lessons from an expert, my little grand-niece, Emma, and she has indicated a few things which Jesus may have meant.

The first thing which strikes me is the sense of wonder. Emma can go: 'Ohooo', over something we take for granted, like the light in the fridge. But she doesn't only wonder once; she can wonder over and over at the same thing. Where an adult would get bored by repetition and say: 'Oh, not again!', a child is more likely to say: 'Do it again!' One day I was trying to distract Emma, and I quoted a little verse which I had heard Geordie Hanna use in an interview with David Hammond:

Up to my nose and down she goes,
and she never stops till she hits my toes,
and heigh-ho she's a dandy!

I didn't explain to Emma that it was like a hymn to a well-known black beverage, but she loved it anyway, and I had to repeat it every day, and every day she beamed as if she was hearing it for the first time.

But perhaps the greatest lesson she taught me was when her mammy brought her to see the parochial house. She had enjoyed running up the long hallway, and when it was time to go home she stopped at the door to say bye-bye. Her mammy said: 'Are you not going to give your uncle Oliver a big kiss?' I wasn't prepared for what happened next, in spite of having once played in goals for Lavey Minors against Desertmartin. Emma didn't pause or lean back on her heels, or give me any warning. She just launched herself without restraint, and it was all I could do to stop her.

'Now that,' I said, 'is what Jesus meant'. Emma didn't pick a spot where she could stop in front of me. Nor did she envisage a line drawn half-way between us where we could meet on a fifty-fifty basis, if we both jumped together. No. It was a question of total trust, of taking off with no holding back: 'Here I come, ready or not'. If we were to become like little children, would we give and not count the cost, trust in our own trust and not worry too much about the consequences?

Battery

I once spoke to a nun from Belfast about changes in religious life. She lived in a small community in an ordinary street. The older impression of religious life was of nuns who worked in school or hospital during the day, but could retire to the seclusion of their convent in the evening. Now, the small house alongside ordinary families has created a new relationship with people. The neighbours' children run in and out at any time of the day, and show an interest in what the Sisters are doing.

A little girl – about three years old – came into the Sisters' prayer room while the Sister was praying. The little girl looked up at the crucifix on the wall, and then looked up at the Sister until she got her attention. 'Sister,' she said, 'put a battery in Jesus and he'll talk to you'.

At one level, the story just gives us a bit of social history about a child's expectation of dolls in the nineteen-nineties, but at another level, the child's expectation made me think about our own expectations of Jesus. When we kneel to pray, with or without the help of a visual aid, are we hoping for a magical intervention, or are we making ourselves available for a real living relationship with Jesus, as a person, and as the Lord of our lives?

There is another story of Jesus speaking from the cross which I find quite intriguing. St Francis was praying in the old ruined church of San Damiano in Assisi when he heard Jesus speaking to him from the crucifix: 'Go, Francis, and build up my Church, which as you see is falling into ruins'. The first application was to the old ruined church, and Francis began to repair it with his own hands. But the fuller meaning had to do with the renewal of the people and the spiritual life of the Church, and the rest of Francis' story concerns that.

During a visit to Assisi I discovered how St Francis came to hear the message of Jesus. Jesus didn't speak to him out of the blue, without preparation. If Jesus did speak to us out of the blue, we probably wouldn't hear him – for the simple reason that we're usually not listening. When Francis heard the message of Jesus, it was after months of prayer, during which Francis prayed every day: 'All highest, glorious God, cast your light into the darkness of my heart. Give me right faith, firm hope, perfect love and deep humility, with wisdom and perception, O Lord, that I may do what is truly your holy will.'

Maybe the message of Jesus for Francis was there all the time: part of the fabric of his life, of God's plan for him. But only the prayer of Francis, the daily listening, the openness to God's will, brought the words of Jesus into focus, like a photograph being developed, or the volume being turned up on a very personal wavelength. Jesus doesn't need a new battery. Maybe we do.

Hands

The weekend before Christmas, people were leaving in toys for families who might be in need of them. They were all shapes and sizes. Some were bravely scuffed, some very well kept, some completely new, still in their wrappings. And then there was a beautifully made doll's kitchen dresser, crafted in wood, fitted together, and hand-painted. There were plastic cups and saucers and all sorts of things to go on the shelves or in the bottom sliding door section. It was about two feet high – just perfect for working at if you were a small person sitting or kneeling on the floor.

The young couple who left it in to the parochial house could have been Mary and Joseph. They arrived out of the night and left a warmth behind them with the toys. He was the carpenter, plier of a trade whose history takes us back to where heaven and earth met in a holy family supported by the work of human hands. She was the wife and the mother.

I thought about the doll's dresser afterwards: about the thought that was behind it, about the planning of it, about the making of it and the painting of it. I thought of skill put at the service of giving, hands at the service of heart. The thought still warms me. Hands are amazing. I remember the childlike wonder with which Brian Keenan looked at his own freed hands at the press conference when he came home from the Lebanon. 'A hand can be made into a fist,' he said, 'to destroy', and he clenched his own fist and looked at it. 'A hand can hold a baby,' he said, and he opened out his own hands, and wondered at the gentleness and compassion the human heart is capable of.

The act that destroys and the act that creates or heals follow the same steps: the thought, the planning, the execution. The hands that have the skill to build are the same hands that can be used for destruction. In reality the hand is only a sign: it is the person who is open or closed; it is the person who decides to destroy or to create, to be for life or to be for death.

For some people that decision is comparatively easy: they have a gift of faith, and an instinct for God's way of working and for God's way of looking at things which makes it natural for them to create and to heal. They know the right way to go, even when it is at great cost. Thank God, we have heard many of them during years of strife calling for forgiveness and not revenge. Their anguish underlines the message of God. Not everyone is so blessed. If the sheer weight of horror leaves you tortured and confused, hold on to one thing: it is better to heal than to hurt; it is better to build than to destroy.

The Rocktown Road

One Thursday in May 1996, on a visit home, I noticed that the Road Services had been patching the Rocktown Road. A bracket of tarmacadam held the 90 degree corner securely in place at Davy's gap, with the fresh surface extending about an equal distance on either side of the corner. Davy Elliott is no longer with us, but the fresh tarmacadam in some way highlighted what was definitely his place, where we might meet him and the spotty dog as we came home from school. As I continued down the road, I was reading the landmarks of our schooldays.

I passed through Kellystown, round the corner at the wood gate, and came to Farrells' loanin'. Then came Milligans' loanin', and what was

Milligans' new house. The next farmyard was Patrick Kelly's – he used an old cut-down car like a kind of jeep, for the sort of work that suits a four-wheel drive nowadays. In some part of my unconscious it will always be Patrick Kelly's, even though O'Kanes have new houses there now. After the old wallsteads I came to Jack McKee's. Jack often drew home turf for us out of Ballinahone, and he could coax amazing power and acceleration out of an old Fordson, as if it were a horse that had been souped up on fresh corn and cajoled and threatened to give of its best and a bit more.

The Rocktown Road was never just a road for us as we went to school, even though we probably could identify every stone and pothole. It wasn't a line on a map. It was more like a procession, a peopled experience, alive with the characters we used meet, day by day, as we came and went to the more formal setting for what would now be referred to as a broad and balanced curriculum. I don't think we ever consciously adverted to the curriculum of the Rocktown Road, where we learned about the busy world of the locality, and the diversity of neighbours who attended different places of worship but who cut the same turf and mowed the same corn, and dug with the same or similar spade, if not with the same foot.

At this turning point in our history, perhaps it's a good thing to be reminded that physical or political geography is not just a matter of territory to be claimed, or of numbers to be counted. The important thing is that the whole place, like the Rocktown Road, is peopled with a variety of characters who have a marvellous potential for enriching each other's lives, as our early years were enriched with the sound and colour and texture of Jack McKee's old Fordson and Davy and the spotty dog.

Pope John XXIII

It was raining heavily in Rome on the morning of October the 11th, 1962. It had rained all night, with thunder and lightning. As the clouds began to clear, Pope John XXIII began his Mass at about half past six. He was calm and serene by nature and by prayer and faith, but he surely must have felt a special thrill of excitement. This was the day when he would enter St Peter's among the assembled bishops of the Catholic world and the leaders of other Christian Churches and world religions, to open the Second Vatican Council.

As a young student in Maynooth I felt the ripples of that excitement all during the Council and afterwards. Vatican II wasn't just the articulation of the Church's tradition for our generation: it was the opening of the windows to let God's creative Spirit blow through. One of Pope John's personal dreams was that the Council would not only work on the conditions of the life of the Catholic Church, but 'would also produce another result: the coming together in one body of the whole of Christ's mystical flock' – though that work might not be complete until 'that blessed time when we close all our doors, and advance together, singing Hosannas, to Paradise'.

Meantime, he set the Council on a course which emphasised many aspects of faith which would find an echo in the hearts of all Christians. The documents of the Council described the Church, not just as an organisation, but as an organic unity, drawing its reality and its perfection from Jesus Christ, its head, and as a community of real people, struggling with their imperfections: the Pilgrim People of God – 'ecclesia semper reformanda' – the Church always in need of reform. The importance of the Scriptures was proclaimed, with the challenging quotation from St Jerome: 'Ignorance of the Scriptures is ignorance of Christ'.

The Council addressed the issues of modern society: issues like social and economic inequality, and peace on earth. Pope John himself gave an account of the original inspiration for the Council coming to him during a conversation with Cardinal Tardini, Secretary of State, about the troubles of the modern world and what the Church could do to help the cause of peace and harmony. At this time in our own history, it is poignant to recall the words of the Vatican Council's document on the Church in the Modern World: 'Peace will never be achieved once and for all, but must be built up continually'.

Granny Bradley

Strabane, where I lived for seventeen years, is a meeting place of roads and rivers. It used to be a meeting place of railways also. Strabane was the key railway junction for people and goods travelling between Derry and Dublin, and between Tyrone and Donegal. I find the idea of the railway junction fascinating. The junction is not where you are going; it's where you change direction to get to where you are going.

I remember travelling from Dublin to Killarney by train, and arriving at Limerick Junction. A faithful old railwayman stood on the platform as the train pulled in, and shouted: 'Kerry train; Kerry train!' Then, as the doors opened and people spilled out on to the platform, that simple place of transition took on the energy of an international airport. Whether it's Strabane or Limerick Junction, the meeting place of the railway lines or the rivers or the roads is important because it is a turning point on the journey. Coming to the crossroads means facing a time of decision – it means choosing your direction.

On our journey, the destination is important: where we're travelling to. But vitally important also is who we're travelling with. On our journey of faith, our destination is to belong to God. We need company and support on our journey; we need people of faith to surround us. Among the great people of faith who guided me on my own journey as I grew up was Granny Bradley, my mother's mother. My grandfather, Paddy Bradley, was station master at Knockloughrim, on the Derry Central Railway.

When we went for our annual outing to Portrush and Portstewart – which we referred to collectively as 'the Port' – we'd leave on the train from Knockloughrim. A few days beforehand, we'd visit Granny Bradley, and we'd say, in some excitement: 'Granny, we're going to the Port'.

Granny would always reply: 'That's great, because I owe two shillings to St Anthony'. She'd entrust the two shilling piece to us, and when we'd arrive on the big day at Portstewart, our mother would see to it that we went immediately to the church to present the coin as Granny had instructed us.

I'm not sure Granny would have approved when two shillings became 10p, and I don't know what she would have made of the euro. It was after her death that we eventually realised what she had been up to, and it had nothing to do with money. When she gave us the two shilling bit and the errand to fulfil, it wasn't just that Granny was very fond of St Anthony, which no doubt she was. More importantly, she was making sure that we wouldn't go for our day at the seaside without visiting a church and saying a prayer. She was concerned with our faith journey, and our mother was her willing accomplice.

Frank Crilley*

My father and his first cousin Frank had never met. Frank lived in Canada, in Saint John, New Brunswick, and for years we had lost contact with the Canadian branch of the family. Then I got an opportunity to visit Saint John, and I went to see Frank in his apartment in the older part of the town. As he led the way into his livingroom, I was amazed at the resemblance to my father, and Frank obviously recognised family features in me too, for he said: 'You needn't tell me you're a Crilley – you couldn't hide it if you tried'.

Frank Crilley was a character worth meeting. He had worked for years on the docks in Saint John,

* Our Canadian cousins spell the name with an 'e'.

and there were many stories about his exploits. Once, while unloading bananas from a ship, he was bitten by a poisonous Tarantula spider. The local newspaper reported the incident and said: 'Typically, Crilley survived and the spider didn't'.

Frank didn't just resemble my father in his physical features; they both had a deep awareness of human rights and fairness. Frank inherited a directness of approach which led him to speak out about injustices in the treatment of the dockers, and he became deeply involved in the trade union movement, first at local and later at national level. His commitment to his fellow workers cost him dearly, both in terms of the struggle for justice, and also eventually in terms of his physical health.

A train carrying dangerous chemicals arrived in the docks. One container was smoking, and seemed to have a leak. The dockers refused to handle it, believing it to be dangerous. The employers insisted that it was safe and would have to be moved. Frank said he wouldn't ask any docker to approach the container until it was checked for safety, and he said he would go down himself and check it. It proved to be unsafe, and the escaping chemicals left him with a very serious lung condition, which eventually killed him.

When I met him, Frank hadn't gone to church for years. I didn't ask him about it, but he told me that he couldn't stomach seeing men on Sunday presenting themselves as pillars of the church, whom he knew during the week as heartless employers wringing the last penny out of the dockers he represented. Their appearance on Sunday was too much of a contradiction with what he experienced of them as a trade union negotiator.

After his death, one of my cousins asked me if I was sad about Frank. 'I miss Frank,' I said, 'but I'm not sad about him. Frank was a man of self-sacrifice and integrity. I am sad about us: committed church people who are so capable of compromise that we can drive away men of Frank's calibre.'

Liam Miller

Liam Miller was a maker of beautiful books. He published modern poetry, like the works of Thomas Kinsella, and he published ancient epics of Ireland and of Wales. His own company was the Dolmen Press, and the mark of his hand could be seen on the little Cuala Press of the Yeats connections. His achievements were many, and yet when you list them you have not begun to describe the man we knew.

He was a man of precision. I remember sitting with Sean O'Boyle in Liam's home in Mountrath while we discussed possible designs for a new book. Liam never talked in the abstract: out would come sheets of paper and typescale, and the possibilities were measured and visualised and decisions were made. No detail ever seemed too much bother to this great man. And he was a great man, the father, or maybe grandfather figure of Irish publishing in our time.

He was a man of depth and of warmth. Some of the most delightful memories of Liam Miller come from the annual Frankfurt Book Fair: the conversation, the humour, the shared experiences. There was the Sunday when Liam purloined the Missal and Lectionary from the Collins stand at the bookfair because we had neglected to provide ourselves with the books we needed for the celebration of Mass in English in this German city. There was the biting cold, one early morning, when Liam almost dragged us through sidestreets to join in worship in German in a little local church which had taken his fancy on a previous visit.

There was the night we were refused admission to a pub where Liam wanted us to hear a famous brass band. We'd just had spaghetti in an Italian cafe, with a glass of wine, but Liam's enthusiasm for the brass band and his – and our – high spirits, like children let out for the evening, convinced the doorman that we had already had far too much to drink.

My own special memory of Liam at the Frankfurt Book Fair comes from another evening. It was the first year, I think, that I had gone to Frankfurt, and Sean O'Boyle and Liam and I had gone out for an evening meal. Liam was wearing a fine light grey poloneck sweater, and I happened to say that it looked very well on him, which it did. I forgot all about that part of the conversation as the evening went on, in the midst of a rich mixture of literary anecdotes and other stories which might not bear retelling. But the next morning, when we came down to breakfast in our hotel, Liam carried in the poloneck sweater and presented it to me, as a souvenir, he said, of my first visit to Frankfurt. It was a typical act of spontaneous generosity.

It was only long afterwards that it struck me that Liam's persevering attention to detail, and the precision with which he approached each book design and each publishing project, was an expression of that same generosity of character.

Jim O'Sullivan

Jim O'Sullivan suited his beard. The streaks of grey, some darker, some lighter, told the story of years of suffering borne without bitterness, and the bushy sweep of it gave to his face the character of an Old Testament prophet. Even if you only saw Jim once, you couldn't forget him easily.

Jim was a man of recognition. Easily recognised himself, he was always recognising other people, and when Jim met you, you felt recognised. The head would go back, he'd embrace you with those deep eyes, and he'd smile a smile of satisfaction as if you'd really made his day. When he put words to all that, it was simply to say in the Derry City idiom: 'What about ye?' I remember Jim once telling me that it would no longer be common practice in Derry to say 'Peace be with you' at the sign of peace at Mass. In future, he said, when people exchanged the ritual handshake, they would give it local life and flavour by saying 'What about ye?'

When Jim wasn't recognising or being recognised, he was usually sharing recognition of something worthwhile, something that extended the horizons of life. Many people, through contact with Jim, came to know of Jean Vanier and the L'Arche communities of the mentally handicapped; of the Little Sisters of Jesus and their contact with the Travelling People; of the Charismatic Renewal Movement; of places like Corrymeela and the growing warmth between Christian denominations which they symbolised and promoted.

Jim had the happy knack of helping his friends to see the presence of God in people or places or things which previously had seemed merely pagan or empty of meaning. I will never forget his reaction to the great pre-Christian burial place of Newgrange in the Boyne Valley. It was snowing that day as we drove up to it, and the office was just being closed, so that we couldn't get in. It wasn't often that bureaucracy got the better of Jim, but even in defeat he was savouring the vision of this place where the burial chambers at the heart of the mound, unseen and for the present inaccessible, lay in the darkness of the earth in the shape of a cross. Five thousand years was a little step from the Boyne people's light conquering darkness, as the sun rose over a wintry Newgrange, to the light of Jim's optimism that evening as we shivered our way back to the car through the sleet.

Newgrange seemed a fitting symbol for Jim. He was a man of the underground, always discovering and sharing the life that was going on in hidden places among what were called insignificant people. He was like the old countryman who divined the water for us in my childhood and told my father where to sink the well. He knew where it was at.

RWANDA SEQUENCE

The Music of What Happens

Fionn Mac Cumhaill, one of the great warriors of the Irish story-telling tradition, said that his favourite music was the music of what happens. That is no surprise, coming from a man of action, but there is a more anguished music: the music of the aftermath of what happens.

I experienced something of that music after the massacres in Rwanda in August 1994. I was with a group associated with the Irish development agency, Trócaire. We drove up from Burundi through the mountains into the South-west of Rwanda. Down in the narrow valleys we could see the light green of the tea crop, a crop that would never be harvested because there was no-one to harvest it. Many were dead; many more were refugees in their own or neighbouring countries. Whatever madness had overtaken that beautiful country left no-one untouched – victims, perpetrators, survivors – all were mutilated beyond recognition, some wounded physically, but most emotionally and personally.

In the aftermath of conflict we are tempted to ask, first, whose fault it was, and then who won and who lost. But the questions are futile. Blame will not bring back the dead, and victory or defeat are not a basis for retrospective justification. Compassion is what is relevant, for those on all sides who have suffered or who have lost their loved ones:

God, our Father,
be patient with us.
You made us rich, and happy, and beautiful.
You looked on your creation
and you saw that it was good.

But we mutilate the beauty of your world.
We turn riches into poverty
and happiness into pain.

Help us to change,
to care passionately,

and yet to be care-free,
to have compassion on the world,
to forgive,
that we may be forgiven.
Amen.

The Darkness of Hunger

A few years back I met a singer in Strabane, County Tyrone. I was based there, and he had come to sing at the town's summer festival. His name was Charlie Lansborough, and he became very popular in Ireland. One of the songs which made him popular was called 'What Colour is the Wind?' The singer looked at the world through the eyes of a blind child, whose father communicates the splendour of the world through colour associations. It is not just things which have colours, but human experience and emotions as well. Gold is the colour of love.

I had never thought of asking what colour is hunger, until I visited Rwanda. I was staying with the Medical Missionaries of Mary at a refugee camp at Cyanika in South-west Rwanda. About eighty thousand people were living in little huts made from branches, crowded together over the hillsides.

At night, the hillsides were in darkness. A few little points of light showed where a fire had been lit outside a hut. The Medical Missionary Sisters told us that no food aid had arrived for the past ten days. When food came, the little cooking fires would be seen at all the huts. Meanwhile, the darkness indicated hunger on a massive scale. The image of the dark hillsides has remained with me as a strong visual memory ever since, and the colour of hunger is black.

Lord,
cast your light
into the darkness of our hearts.
Help us to see beyond the surface of things
to the reality that lies beneath.
Help us to see the colours of joy and sorrow,
of suffering and sympathy.

Help us to care for those who hunger,
and help us to hunger and thirst
for justice and peace in the world.
Amen.

Building Bricks

My mother grew up in a little railway station on the Derry Central railway, where my grandfather was the local station master. Because of that, the red and yellow brick of the railway architecture of the early twentieth century is part of my visual memory. The little railway station still stands, though the railway itself is long gone. The neat brick building speaks of an era when things were made to a set standard, when trains ran to time, and everything was orderly.

Travelling through Rwanda, I found an echo of the world of red and yellow brick building which was home to my mother's people. In each parish or diocesan centre we visited, there was an orderly compound, with the church, the school, the priests' house, and perhaps a monastery or convent – all built with the local brick which was a feature of Rwandan construction, and which also reflected the tradition of the German and Belgian colonial powers who had ruled there before Rwandan independence.

In August of 1994 the infrastructures of Rwanda had been torn apart. There was no telephone system, no electricity, and scarcely any safe drinking water. The neat and orderly construction of the red brick buildings stood in anguished paradox against the confusion of a suffering society.

Lord,
In the Church and in the world,
with the best of intentions,
so often we build the external structures;
we place the brick, the stone, the steel,
and expect to impose our order and our shape
on the world in which we live.

We expect the work of our hands
to give us permanence.

Teach us to build relationships,
to labour slowly and sensitively,
to allow structures to evolve,
not to a predetermined plan,
but into a vision that is shared,
that we can realise together.

Walking on the Blood

We had spent a few days at the refugee camps in Cyanika in South-west Rwanda. The roads to the North had just been opened. We prepared to go to the Capital, Kigali. The Medical Missionary Sisters gave us a large saucepan full of cooked rice, white rice, marked on top with a generous spoonful of red jam. It was our food for the journey.

We didn't eat the rice until we arrived in Kigali, at the Mille Collines Hotel, the Hotel of the Thousand Hills, once the Sabena Airlines flagship tourist accommodation. There was no electricity in the hotel, no telephones, no drinking water. Water for flushing the toilets was carried upstairs by hand from what remained in the swimming pool. There was, of course, no question of cooking or serving meals. We ate our rice cold, and were thankful for it.

The whole experience has remained with me to this day, graphically imprinted on my memory. But one part of it stands out above all the rest. When I got to my room, by the light of torch and candle, I had to pick my steps across the floor to avoid the pools of congealed blood on the carpet before I could get to bed. I eventually slept, but I couldn't put out of my mind the images of what must have happened in that place. The tense aftermath of violence seemed to hang in the air.

Lord,
forgive us for our hatred and cruelty,
for the violence we do to one another,
for seeking revenge
rather than reconciliation.

Forgive us also for our inaction,
when we allow ourselves
to be paralysed by fear,
by sectarian hatred,
by our own selfishness.
Help us to love even our enemies –
especially our enemies.

Amen.

Harvest Restored

After ten very intense days travelling around Rwanda in the aftermath of massacre and war, we got a lift on a Canadian plane out of Kigali airport. Even though the airport showed the scars of war, and there was none of the usual airport bustle, the new military administration had arranged for a rudimentary departure check-in. Two young men stood each by a table, on which intending passengers – nine of us – had to place our cases for examination.

As I opened my case, the young official looked down and said: 'Is that your Bible?' 'Yes,' I said. Then he asked, 'Can you give me a word from the Bible for my country at this time?' I replied that on our journey the day before down to Kibungo, we had talked of a text from Joel 2:25, where the Lord said: 'I will restore the years which the locust has devoured'.

'Thank you,' he said, and he seemed genuinely moved. Then he said: 'I too will give you a word from the Bible, and he quoted from Genesis 28: 'Know that I am with you and will keep you wherever you go'. Then he threw out his arms and gave me a great charismatic hug. It was something I have never experienced at an airport check-in before or since, and it filled me with hope.

Lord,

we are people of little expectation,
and of little ambition for what really matters.
We expect little good to come out of Nazareth,
or out of Kigali,
or out of Belfast or Baghdad.

Help us to know that your goodness and love
lie hidden deep down
in the most unexpected places.
Help us to accept
a word of encouragement

or an act of kindness,
even when it comes from a source
we'd rather not acknowledge.

Amen.